Proof of Stake is tenderly radical, a the Miltonic oak, the anti-Miltonic lost loved one close against his chest as he soars through continents, continents, climates, colonialisms and profit motives, seeking both to register her and protect her from the shitty banns of human time. This is virtuosic writing that abjures writing, naming that abjures naming, a history that abjures histories, and finally abjures its own virtuosity. Yet the love and the desire to continue loving can never be rubbed out. The poem concludes not with consolation but with the resolution to go on with this devotional quest, this simultaneous making-unmaking, to escape form and "widen the aperture... Dark, more dark."

– Joyelle McSweeney

"How do we continue when so much depends/ On stable interfaces communicating?" With *Proof of Stake*, Charles Valle produces a text of mourning wherein the unspeakable and unacceptable loss of his infant daughter, Vivian, entwines with the inheritances that would have been hers – the unstable interfaces of contemporary life born of colonialism, racism, and global capitalism. That is to say, the inheritances that are ours. Line-by-line, phrase-by-phrase, Valle, who knows there is no real relating to the living or the dead without attending "histories wrought with erasure," develops a "poetics of grief," "An integral/ Lower limit memory/ Upper limit intertextuality." Here, the limits of memory carry the beloved as detail, as tender subject of address, as name. Drawing on textual material as varied as the late sixteenth-century colonial *Boxer Codex* and today's hashtags, *Proof of Stake's* upper limit opens to the suffering, past and present, of all living things. How do we continue? Diamond-scarred with the integrity and generosity earned only by un-speakable grief, Valle realizes a way: "If not in outrage, then in poetry/ If not in poetry, then in song." *Proof of Stake* is that poetry, is that song.

– Karla Kelsey

Charles Valle's *Proof of Stake* is the distillation of "desolation after song." A book-length elegy mourning an inconceivable loss to which the speaker is tethered, it as much asserts and interrogates languages, politics, histories, memories, and poetics. Imbued with heartbreak and rage, Valle, with "the portability of grief," travels in search of transcendence to return to a reconfigured landscape of his making.

– Joseph O. Legaspi

"And when I think of the phrases unturned" in the aftermath of loss, Charles Valle writes, "I am reminded of the histories / Wrought with erasure." How does one move forward, how does one write, when "grief has become so decentralized" that our shared languages for compassion burn in the ashen husk of colonial afterimage? Valle's *Proof of Stake: An Elegy* reanimates the elegy form from the detritus and syntagma of global capitalism's death-drive, localizing its song of grief, anger, and compromised beauty in a heartbreaking apostrophe to his daughter Vivian. Written in the dark heart of pandemic, Valle's cathartic work reimagines "the possibilities of desolation / after song," in which the curated artifice of "the global" collapses under the weight of quarantine malaise, generational trauma, and the cruel burials language enacts on the dead and the marginal. Where the voice is unwoven from its hold on human contact, a sound of mourning rises in the apertures where history leaks out and soaks the ground of the representable in a profligate futility. Epistolary modes fail, accidental hashtags fail, lyric beauty fails, aestheticized melancholy fails, the very act of writing fails because: "How do we continue when so much depends / On stable interfaces communicating?" Valle explores (and explodes) the polyglossic failure of language to accommodate the unspeakable cadences of grief—at a time when the self-reflexivity of an accelerated historicism blurs the boundaries of the self and the voice—and he pieces together a counternarrative from the shards of an unresolvable debt beyond the corrosive mediation of social-media-speak and the infernal recurrence of colonialism. Where "there are no words / there are words," and *Proof of Stake* compels us to listen to the sound absence carves on the skin of remembrance.

– Jose-Luis Moctezuma

Charles Valle's *Proof of Stake* is at once an elegy for his daughter, a lament for the opaqueness of life, an exploration of one of the greatest themes of poetry—the failure of poetry—and ultimately a questioning of what it is to be human. As he sits on the floor of the hospital where his daughter comes into then out of life, we travel the corridors of his mind, bearing witness to the absurdities, cruelties, and erasures that link us to each other and the past: from those of a person's private grief to cultures flattened by conquistadors, histories never written, forgotten, left to decompose, or translated into the bloodshed of Hollywood catharsis....The language of this meditation is simple, its insights profound and deeply felt: a powerful expression of our shared existence—a poetic triumph.

– Steve Tomasula

Charles Valle's poetry collection *Proof Of Stake* is an impassioned and necessary exploration of grief and mourning. Valle grieves the loss of his child, Vivian, while also confronting the confounding world of past-present colonial occupations with acts of deep resistance. In this fierce lyric sequence, he confronts racial injustice, and the fragile and violent present affairs of the human and natural world. Understandably, throughout the book, Valle's poems reside in the inconsolable space where finding words to articulate deep loss may be impossible but he summons them for a function and a powerful address to Vivian whose death has left him to muddle in the impenetrable space of reaching: "Tumble into words, Vivian. I want/My words to organize around grief/ And contribute to the economy/Of suffering." His economy is in the poem's ability to shape the suffering. In this sequence, we see how the lyric drives the modulations of the speaker into definitions that unearth and absorb deeper meaning from the affairs of the state around the speaker-griever, and allow the him to drop in and out of the world's cruel consumption and exploitation of bodies, of souls, to a greater reckoning with grief.

— Prageeta Sharma

"And when I think of the phrases/unturned,/The lines not breaking, the words/That will never ring for you,/Vivian, I am reminded of the histories/wrought with erasure," are among the astonishing lines that open Charles Valle's *Proof of Stake*, a book-length elegy about his late daughter Vivian, who passed away shortly after her birth in 2011, and to whom his long poem is addressed. At once *Howl*, *Somebody Blew Up America*, and *The Disintegration Loops* for our pandemic and new Yellow Peril era, Valle's extraordinary poem is further proof of the stake that 21st century experimental BIPOC poets'—including Kamau Brathwaite, M. NourbeSe, Fred Wah, Jordan Abel, Douglas Kearney, Barbara Jane Reyes, and Aldrin Valdez—continue to claim in the elegy to explore and create powerful new modes of grieving and protest. "Let me tell you about/ my poetics of grief", Valle's speaker offers, mourning Vivian's absence yet absorbing "the opposite of decisive moments", so that they might "invent a new plasticity of language,.../And strike these words to widen the aperture/To blur the background, all that baggage/In buttery bokeh, unrecognizable/Dark". Let me tell you this about Charles Valle's debut book of poetry: *Proof of Stake* breaks new ground for the elegy, and your heart along with it. A brilliant, moving, and unforgettable work.

— Paolo Javier

PROOF OF STAKE AN ELEGY

PROOF OF STAKE AN ELEGY

CHARLES VALLE

FONO
GRAF

FONOGRAF EDITIONS
2021

Fonograf Editions
Portland, OR

First Edition, First Printing

FONO11

Published by Fonograf Editions
www.fonografeditions.com

For information about permission to reuse any material from this book, please con-
tact Fonograf Ed. at info@fonografeditions.com.

Distributed by Small Press Distribution
SPDBooks.org

ISBN # 978-1-7344566-6-0

LCCN: 2021932242

For Vivian,

Kathleen, and

Avelina

Memories shorn

Leaves falling again

Birches, maples

Poplars, those diamond scars

Bursting forth. Oaken and

Ashen projections of future lives

Shorn or sheared

A shared understanding of a

Quasi clusterfuck

Full of twists

Populus pulp for the pressing

Perfect bound for the words

You will never read, Vivian.

Stories unfinished, fragments and all

And when I think of the phrases unturned,

The lines not breaking, the words

That will never ring for you,

Vivian, I am reminded of the histories

Wrought with erasure.

I am standing atop a cornice

Of a mountain I've never climbed

The escarpment unfolds and I am terrified

The escarpment unfolds and I want to hurl

My body and create

An avalanche, Vivian

I want my thoughts to cascade,

Tumble into words, Vivian. I want

My words to organize around grief

And contribute to the economy

Of suffering. I want my grief

To go viral and not shelter

In place. An imagined pandemic

Of mourning exponentially

Rising, then falling

This is what I thought

Our lives would be

Going through motions

Checking boxes

Striking through lists like

Crossing the Brooklyn Bridge

Strolling through Buckingham Palace

Watching the sun rise over Angkor Wat

Or descending on Machu Picchu

All silhouettes and golden light bathing

Desolate ruins of empires

This is the age of the desolation tourism

Or, this is the age of disintegration voyeurism

Or, this is the age of experiential inequity

What stage capitalism?

How do we unfuck ourselves?

Can we place faith in such

Incremental change when the men

Behind the men behind the invisible

Hands maintain such solid grips

On the stage curtains? There are backdrops

In front of the backdrops, scrims

In front of scrims, grand drapes becoming

False proscenia. The production

So complex, the audience is forced

Into performance, the chorus into stage hands,

The producers are picking up trumpets and trombones,

The financiers are conducting the orchestra,

The actors are changing directions. Even the absurdity

Unfolding in front of the false proscenium

Is confused for reality

The central banks have succeeded

In redefining the Theatre of Cruelty.

The confusion so perfect

The audience is too busy tapping

Hashtags instead of throwing tomatoes

Or burning down the proscenium arch

They keep killing Black people and I need the WiFi password

They're bombing the wedding party again and I need to charge
my devices

They put us in lockdown again and I'm at 1%

$SPX wins again. All time highs.

We're dying here #pleasesendnudes

How can we break free

From manufactured dissent

Sanctioned by the DNC,

Powered by FAANG?

How do empires fall?

Think of lineage now

Think of diasporas and Reconquista

Oaken and ashen histories

Shorn or sheared

Stories scribbled on Chinese paper

Not populus pulp, but mulberry bark,

Perhaps, hemp rags, the detritus of fish nets

Ts'ai Lun and his guarded recipe

And maybe this is the story of adoption and penetration

Maybe this is the story of mistaking innovation

For iteration

How paper travelled west

Then north before heading back

Oh, you lovely caryatids

With your tongue-tied titty twisters

Oh, cacophonous caliphate

Recalling Ibrahim in verse

Or Abraham in song

In the cave of double caves

Double tombs become sanctuaries

Basilica becomes mosque becomes synagogue

A cenotaph here

A minaret there

Build more words

And cut a quill

And angle to a point

How paper killed parchment

And erasure

For the dye bleeding through dried pulp

Implies transparency in transaction

Implies an imagined permanence

For what is a smudge on dead skin

Mistakes

Mistakes

Misshapes

And my mind is smudgy pulp

All flayed remnants of brown skin, incoherent

Thoughts, projections of paternal aptitude, the detritus

Of hope, macerated

Pressed and dried

There are no words

There are words

There are no words

There are utterances

There are the incomplete silences

Guttural grunts and groaning

An emptiness like nothing

I've ever felt

The sensation of phantom limbs

Where limbs lay dormant

Parts of me died each day with you Vivian

Parts of me want to cover my body in your story

In cuneiform, say, in Assyrian,

In some dead language

In more indecipherable glyphs

A pictogram, perhaps, of how I lost

My tongue or how I want to never let

You go with my phantom limbs

There is an emotional debt accrued

In grief, compounded daily by wordless songs,

Atonal instrumentals

Unstable harmonies leading

To more guttural grunts and groans

Oh, you lovely caryatids

with your tongue-tied titty twisters

Oh, cacophonous caliphate

My emotions are disguised as Byzantine generals

Traitorous and treacherous

Surrounding an imagined city

That may or may not be

A clumsy metaphor

for my faculties

An imagined city is under siege

And the generals cannot trust each other

To lay waste or retreat

An imagined city is under siege

And the populists do not know it

Cannot fathom such decimation

Cannot imagine the possibilities

Of desolation after song

Cannot conceive a fault tolerance

Capable of consensus

The populists cannot agree on the value

Of life in their imagined city. Is caring

For the sick and feeding the poor

An imagined human right?

The populists do not speak the same language

All realities a deep fake

The populists cannot agree on the beauty

Or annoyance of populus catkins

Floating like so much fake snow

Gathering in corners, in ramparts

Coalescing as the wind takes them

Children run with arms outstretched

Like little brown planes caught

In a blizzard in slow motion

The babies are breathing in catkins and choking

Engines are sucking them in and dying

Buildings are expanding and contracting

In Beijing, they conceive sex change operations

As populus solutions

Just to stop the fucking things

From producing flying pollen

And there are other solutions

Some more elegant

And others, less so,

Like let's just wait for the population to die

And start anew

Or let's just leave them be

To lose their leaves in their own silence

Much like grief, perhaps

In stages

In waves

Someone is tracking the lower highs,

The lower lows

Someone is anticipating

Such psychological movements

Calling bottoms

Predicting retracements from further waves

And all this analysis is bullshit

In all this analysis, nothing matters

So much as a desire to connect

Once more. I want to become

Epistolary as fuck.

And to think, letters struck

Through become another word birthed

Deletion and transposition conceiving

A new name, another...

You will not be our only child, Vivian

I want to send parcels and postcards

To the Marianas

The Carolines

Palau

Brunei

I want to send an unmarked box

To the Abbasid caliphate

Full of love letters, ship registers, tax returns

I want words to travel

As cascading disruptions

I want words to travel

In divergent paths, in multiple meanings

How we deal with language sharding

Into buildings of hollows

Into neighborhoods full of hollows

A whole fucking city full of hollows

And there are the canonical words in shards

Consumed in curated layers

Extracted

Transformed

Loaded with so much ideological baggage

They are collapsing under the weight

Of their attribution

~~Socialism~~ implies _____

~~Fascism~~ implies _____

~~Capitalism~~ implies _____

And the shards are calcifying with each tweet

Every thread coiling

Unspooling and knot once again

Culture pressed and dried

Think then of the Chinese papermakers

Captured by the caliphate

Bound and willing

Or unbound in conjecture

Those Abbasids knew they had something good

But could they have ever fathomed

How their prisoners would change

The world forever?

Think, then, of other use cases, perhaps

Say, poplar panels for the Mannerists

Elongating limbs and distorting perspectives

As in a circle not a circle

Or a square not a square

Parallelograms in comfort

In grief

And memories are

Foreshortening still

Is trauma receding

Or ready to pounce once more?

Am I at the foot

Or the heart of all these laments?

And already the memories

Are being overwritten

The sharp, jagged edges filed down

More polished

More cinematic

But how do we foreshorten emotions

So that the dullness seems farther?

How do we resurrect the intensity

Of those first few hours

When everything felt too vivid?

#latergram

It's 2011 and I am sitting on the floor

In a hospital hallway. The incandescent buzzing

Moving to the foreground

I do not know

Whether to place my hands on my temples

Or rip out my hair

Genderless scrubs blur by

A cacophony of medical terms burst forth

I try to focus on something before me

And fixate on the geometric shapes

On the newly-waxed floor

Is this cinematic enough?

The incandescent buzzing transitions

Arpeggiated minor chords in heavy reverb

Rising and falling

Moving towards some expected crescendo

That we may or may not endure

And for some time after there were no words

Just emotions articulated through strict serialism

Social interactions mediated through scripted pursed lips

Quivering, the constant negotiation of trying to be

Present, or yielding to the rising effect of being

A spectator to your own conversations

The numbness so encompassing

#nofilter

And the portability of grief is such a wondrous thing

The transit so efficient

Every circumstance so easily succumbing

To tenebristic splendor

The unsettling realism of the eyes you never opened, Vivian,

The lifeless hand that could not grip my trembling fingers

Follow me across continents

From Europe to Asia, the dark

Background persists with single sources of light

Shining on different body parts

One day, it is your perfectly-shaped eyebrows

The next, the meconium spilling out of your nose,

Your mouth. I close my eyes in Cambodia and see

Your hands. I wake up in Iceland and the light focuses

On your chin, your lips. In Singapore, I burn incense

And imagine your voice. In the Philippines, I scatter

Your ashes on the leeward side of hope

And reflection, the prismatic nature of remains

Ashen and oaken, bits of bones

So far removed from any sense of

Purpose or structure

Mourning in residue

The structures of grief pressed

And dried. Textures so indecipherable

They disorient with ease

Emotional glyphs asperating sullied surfaces

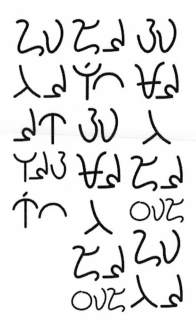

I'm trying to make sense of it all

But the meanings escape as quickly

As the memories form

A scent here

A song there

Feeling you tumble and kick

Through your mother's worn sweater

The ultrasounds like cosmic

Pulses, codes I could never

Decipher, in retrospect

Were there messages

In the space noises?

Nuances lost in stilted poetics

Of remembrance? If only I had faith,

I would embrace divination, or in

Desperation, attend a séance, say,

Or divine meaning in tea leaves

In coffee grounds, in tarot cards

The stars' alignments

In cosmic conjunctions

In retrogrades

Let me tell you

About my poetics of grief

$$\int_{memory}^{intertextuality}$$

An integral

Lower limit memory

Upper limit intertextuality

Some things we will never know

Others we recreate in inadequate

Prototypes. *Failing fast* a euphemism

For bringing ideas to life

Without rigor or discipline

The things in themselves

Such rough translations

They are nearly comical

And everything is an act of translation

And everything slips

Between bounded contexts

Putang ina ko is Tagalog for
I love you

Come mierda y muere is Spanish for
I hope you feel great

Pēdīcābō ego vōs et irrumābō is Latin for
You're right, it must all be God's will

μαλακια is Greek for
Lovely

Domain Driven Design is Geek for
Fuck all y'all

Stakeholder fatigue is business speak for
Back the fuck up

Defund the Police is American for
I want to skullfuck your grandma and eat your babies

Blue Lives Matter is 'Murican for
Just harvesting strange fruit in my poplar grove.

How do we continue when so much depends

On stable interfaces communicating?

If not in outrage, then in poetry

If not in poetry, then in song

How did we get this far, Vivian?

I mean, really,

How did we get here?

How did the poplar panels die

And make way for canvas?

The Mannerists again?

The Caravaggisti?

Was it simply vulgar

Economics?

Regardless, canvas

For the stretching

Followed Reconquista

Jesus in shades of burnt umber

On hemp derivatives

Mohammed in erasure in absence

Prophets and profits

Skein to skein

Baroque is broken after

History's serpentine

                          movements

Like the Portuguese armada

slithering through

The straits of Malacca

Preparing to sack the cities and palaces of the sultanate

The Portuguese infidels' reputations

Preceding them, secured through their piracy

And savagery—sewing dog's ears

On mutilated hostages, perhaps a bit

Too much for the heathens.

I flip through the pages of the Boxer Codex

The Tagalogs

The Visayans

The Negritos

The constituent caricatures

All in such vivid color, Vivian

Your progenitors

The precolonial adornments

Refinements, the weaponry

Such unnatural gestures captured

Bound in Chinese paper

Timeless in reproduction

Mythology blurring deities, demons

Nobles and warriors

Parts of me died each day with you Vivian

Parts of me want to cover my body in your story

In Suyat, say, in Kulitan,

In precolonial script

Diacritics and all

#TBT

1/5

Battle of Mactan, 1521

Silhouettes of Spanish ships anchored far from the shore

The sky and sea are bathed in golden light

Wispy clouds a darker hue

2/5

Ferdinand Magellan leads forty-nine armored men with swords, axes, shields, crossbows, and muskets

Their faces strain as they wade through thigh high water

Details of rocks and coral frame the soldiers

The blue water, so perfectly clear

3/5

Hundreds of natives surround the heavily-armored soldiers

The natives are throwing rocks and spears

Their ferocity contrasting the demoralized faces of the Spanish soldiers

Soldier setting house on fire in foreground

As dozens of houses burn in the background

The smoke obscures the faces

Bottom right, a native, mouth

Agape, as another native lunges

At the soldier, anger in his eyes

A dozen soldiers surround Magellan

In various stages of slaughter

As a large crowd of natives attack

with spears and kampilans

In the center, Magellan on the ground tending

To his bloodied left leg. Natives advancing

To pierce and slice.

#partysover

I think of LapuLapu

Standing in the blood of Magellans' men

And it's hard not to project some trace

Of Hollywood in cathartic bloodshed

And it's hard not to project our 21st century

Concepts of freedom

~~And though he delayed Spanish conquest forty years,~~

~~LapuLapu already knew the horrors of politics and commerce~~

Before Magellan, there were the Hindu and Buddhist and
Muslim elites

Datus and Rajahs

Sultans and Emperors

Demanding fealty, tributes, agreements

LapuLapu was an animist

Some say

LapuLapu was a Muslim

Was he a pirate, a puppet, a pauper, a poet

A pawn or a king?

And what does it matter

Given the chance to slaughter

Foreign invaders with outrageous

Demands? It's the story of the Philippines, Vivian.

Trade stipulations

In religious disguises

Rajah Humabon becomes Don Carlos

Blood compacts misinterpreted

Or so I assume

In 1565, Miguel López de Legazpi left Mexico under order from King Philip II to find the Spice Islands.

The nutmeg, mace, and cloves too irresistible

After burning some Chamorro huts in the Marianas, Legazpi's ships continued west

Befriending Datus and Rajahs on different islands

Until he was challenged by the chief of Cebu

If not by friendship, then by negotiations

If not by negotiations, then by force

Legazpi continued until all the islands

Were under Spanish rule

Lingua franca codified

Catholic conversions the norm

Cultures flattened, their detritus

Transformed, reattributed, disseminated

Via the Manila Galleon trade route

The next couple centuries a blur

Of revolts and uprisings

Dialects dying, social strata crumbling,

Reforming and crystallizing

A fragile 7,000 piece puzzle

So perfect for smashing

In 1896, the Katipunan started the Philippine Revolution. After their secret society was discovered

By the Spanish, the Katipuneros tore their identification

Papers and proceeded to battle the Spanish forces,

Establishing the First Philippine Republic in 1899

Only to be dissolved by the Americans

After the Philippine-American War

More conquest

More gods

More death

This is some of the history that your brother and sister will have to negotiate, Vivian

Empire building⇌Resistance

And it's a stale wind whispering

for change, Vivian

Moar conquest

Moar gods

Moar death

How do we unfuck ourselves?

How do we get out from under the weight of it?

Consider the catenary of our change curves

Derive the secant and tangents

Shock to depression

No denial

No denial

Someone is tracking the higher

Lows, the higher highs

Someone is anticipating

Such psychological movements

Calling for melt ups

$SPX wins again. All time highs.

I'm waiting for a blow off top

But the money printer keeps going

BRRR BRRRRRR BRRRRRRRRR

Bearish engulfing candles

Invalidated daily. And all this analysis is bullshit.

In all this analysis, nothing matters

So much as a desire to connect

Once more

It's 2019 and there's a man who wants me

to go back to where I came from

There's a man who wants to

Call me a _____

And I'm not even a _____

There's a man who wants to

Teach me a lesson on supremacy

It's 2020 and the unctuous dreams

Unravel. The kids are toppling

Statues and monuments of old

Slavers and confederate generals

Some decapitated, some defaced, others

Decomposing in lakes and rivers

Reckoning after reckoning

Oregon is on fire

Michigan is under water

Climate disasters the new norm

The socially-distanced food lines keep growing

Yet increasing less than the billionaires'

Coffers. Everything feels historical

Our empathic stores looted

Moral reserves drained. Essentialness

Always already redefined

And in certain ways, I am grateful

That grief has become so decentralized

That everyone has a stake

In the validation of loss

There are people who want me to believe in one history

They want us to become horribly synchronous again

As if we can ever negotiate

The divide between those in power

And the collection of peoples who mark

Time's passage by paycheck or harvest

I want to find a way out of time

A formless, lifeless photograph, perhaps

The opposite of decisive moments

I want to escape the photographer's gaze

And reorganize the forms, the lines, the landscapes

I want to strike back and destroy the recognizable

Patterns, the letters, the histories

I want to invent a new plasticity of language,

Of movement, of motions, of grief

And strike these words to widen the aperture

To blur the background, all that baggage

In buttery bokeh, unrecognizable

Dark, more dark

Acknowledgments

Thanks to Jeff, Justin, and *Fonograf* for believing in the manuscript and publishing this book. Much appreciation and respect to Andy Mister, whose image graces the cover. Humble and heartfelt gratitude for the lovely blurbs from some of my favorite writers: Paolo Javier, Joyelle McSweeney, Karla Kelsey, Prageeta Sharma, Jose-Luis Moctezuma, Joseph Legaspi, and Steve Tomasula. All of your writing has touched me in different ways over the years. Joyelle and Steve: thank you for encouraging me to finish this manuscript after the initial reading of the first draft. Thank you Notre Dame Creative Writing Program for inviting me out to read in 2019: without your nudge, I would still have a bunch of fragments. Thank you to Pat Schwiebert, the Peace House, and Brief Encounters for helping me find my *new normal*. Thanks to Christina Kubasta and Brain Mill Press for publishing an excerpt from *Proof of Stake*.

Ivan and Olive: you are my everything...I love you!

FONO
GRAF

A registered 501(c)(3) non-profit organization, Fonograf Editions publishes books and records, ones literary in origin. Each release is available in different forms, with a particular focus on the tangible artifact. Previous titles have included *Aloha/irish trees* by Eileen Myles, *The Black Saint and the Sinnerman* by Harmony Holiday, *Live in Seattle* by Alice Notley, *Instrument/Traveler's Ode* by Dao Strom and *Returning the Sword to the Stone* by Mark Leidner. Find a full publication list and more information about the press at: fonografeditions.com.